, Landmarks, and Monuments

# NASA

Tamara L. Britton
**ABDO Publishing Company**

**visit us at**
**www.abdopub.com**

Published by ABDO Publishing Company, 4940 Viking Drive, Edina, Minnesota 55435.
Copyright © 2005 by Abdo Consulting Group, Inc. International copyrights reserved in
all countries. No part of this book may be reproduced in any form without written
permission from the publisher. The Checkerboard Library™ is a trademark and logo of
ABDO Publishing Company.

Printed in the United States.

Cover Photo: Corbis
Interior Photos: Corbis pp. 1, 4, 5, 6-7, 8, 10, 18, 19; Getty Images pp. 14, 20, 21;
    NASA-HQ-GRIN p. 11; NASA-JPL pp. 25, 27; NASA-JSC p. 13;
    NASA-KSC pp. 16, 23; NASA-LaRC p. 9; NASA-MSFC p. 29

Series Coordinator: Heidi M. Dahmes
Editors: Heidi M. Dahmes, Megan M. Gunderson, Jennifer R. Krueger
Art Direction & Maps: Neil Klinepier

### Library of Congress Cataloging-in-Publication Data

Britton, Tamara L., 1963-
    NASA / Tamara L. Britton.
        p. cm. -- (Symbols, landmarks, and monuments)
    Includes index.
    ISBN 1-59197-836-X
        1. United States. National Aeronautics and Space Administration--Juvenile
    literature. I. Title.

TL521.312.B75 2005
354.79'0973--dc22

                                                                    2004057404

# Contents

# NASA

In 1957, the Soviet Union and the United States were locked in the **Cold War**. That year, the Soviets launched a **satellite** into space. The United States did not want to fall behind the Soviet Union in space exploration. Soon, the two nations began a space race.

On October 1, 1958, the National **Aeronautics** and Space Administration (NASA) began operating. In 1961, President John F. Kennedy asked Americans to put a man on the moon by 1970. NASA met the president's challenge. In 1969, Neil Armstrong became the first man to walk on the moon.

*An Apollo 15 astronaut salutes the American flag on the moon.*

4

Since that time, NASA has sent **probes** to Venus and Saturn. It has landed craft on Mars. NASA has played an important role in linking the world with **satellite** communications. And, it has given us knowledge of how to live and work in space.

NASA is a symbol of the possibility of achievement. It is a monument to brave men and women. Many have given their lives to advance our knowledge of space.

*The Kennedy Space Center near Cape Canaveral in Florida*

# Fast Facts

√ The word *astronaut* means "sailor of the stars."

√ During the Apollo 14 mission, Alan B. Shepard became the first man to play golf on the moon.

√ On February 20, 1962, John Glenn orbited Earth aboard *Friendship 7*.

√ On July 17, 1975, the United States and the Soviet Union began working together in space. The United States had already won the space race. And, the Cold War hostilities were lessening. *Apollo 18* and *Soyuz 19* rendezvoused and docked during the Apollo-Soyuz Test Project. This was the first piloted space mission between two countries.

√ After the Apollo program ended, NASA worked on creating a place for living and working in space. Three separate three-man crews used the Skylab space station to study the effects of space on the human body.

√ Skylab 4 was the last manned mission. The crew broke a record by spending 84 days in space! In 1979, Skylab reentered Earth's atmosphere and broke up over Australia.

√ On June 18, 1983, Sally K. Ride became the first U.S. woman in space. The first African American in space was Guion Bluford Jr. on August 30, 1983.

# Timeline

1915 √ President Woodrow Wilson created the National Advisory Committee for Aeronautics (NACA).

1958 √ President Dwight D. Eisenhower signed the National Aeronautics and Space Act. This act created the National Aeronautics and Space Administration (NASA). NASA began operations on October 1.

1961 √ Alan B. Shepard became the first American in space; in a speech on May 25, President John F. Kennedy asked Americans to commit to landing a man on the moon by 1970.

1969 √ Neil Armstrong made the first human footprint on the moon's surface.

1981 √ NASA launched the space shuttle *Columbia* from the Kennedy Space Center.

1986 √ On January 28, the space shuttle *Challenger* exploded 73 seconds after takeoff.

2003 √ The space shuttle *Columbia* broke apart upon reentering Earth's atmosphere.

2004 √ President George W. Bush announced the Vision for Space Exploration Program.

# *Early Efforts*

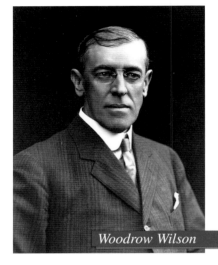

On March 3, 1915, President Woodrow Wilson created the National Advisory Committee for **Aeronautics** (NACA).  NACA used their research findings to improve the performance of airplanes.

In the late 1940s, the United States and the Soviet Union were in the **Cold War**.  Each country was competing to

*Woodrow Wilson*

develop technology that would allow it to explore space.

This competition became known as the space race.  The Soviets took the lead on October 4,

*A model of* Sputnik 1.  Sputnik *is Russian for "companion."*

1957, when they launched *Sputnik 1*. It was the world's first man-made **satellite**.

American scientists had to work quickly to catch up with the Soviets. So on July 29, 1958, President Dwight D. Eisenhower signed the National **Aeronautics** and Space Act. This act created the National Aeronautics and Space Administration (NASA).

On October 1 of that year, NASA took over NACA. The new agency went to work researching manned spaceflight. It also worked to develop and build spacecraft and to explore space.

*NACA developed the wind tunnel for studying aerodynamics. The wind tunnel helped create the swept-back wing design. This wing style allowed Chuck Yeager to break the sound barrier in 1947.*

# *The Space Race*

In 1958, the United States pulled even with the Soviets when the army launched *Explorer 1*. It was the first U.S. **satellite** in space. Later that year, NASA took over space exploration from the military.

NASA soon began the Pioneer program. *Pioneer 1* was the first spacecraft NASA launched. On March 3, 1959, *Pioneer 4* became the first U.S. craft to leave Earth's orbit.

Landing a man on the moon was still not possible. NASA first needed to know if astronauts could survive in space. So, NASA began Project Mercury.

*The mission Mercury-Redstone 3 put the first American into space. NASA allowed the Mercury astronauts to name their own spacecraft. So, Alan B. Shepard named his* Freedom 7.

The program developed hardware and technology that would help astronauts survive outside of Earth's atmosphere.

In the middle of this hard work, the Soviets were also making strides. In April 1961, Yury Gagarin became the first man in orbit on *Vostok 1*. But, the Americans were not far behind. On May 5, 1961, Alan B. Shepard became the first American in space. He took a 15-minute flight in *Freedom 7*.

*The original Project Mercury astronauts. Front row* (left to right): *Walter M. Schirra, Donald Slayton, John Glenn, and Scott Carpenter. Back row* (left to right): *Alan B. Shepard, Virgil "Gus" Grissom, and Leroy Gordon Cooper Jr.*

But, Americans knew second place was not good enough. On May 25, 1961, President John F. Kennedy addressed Congress. This became known as the Urgent National Needs speech. In it, the president asked Americans to commit to landing a man on the moon before 1970.

The president's speech energized NASA's scientists. So, NASA began the Gemini program. Gemini scientists worked to develop a craft in which two men could orbit Earth.

Over the next few years, the Gemini astronauts practiced **rendezvous** and **docking**. They tested human endurance in space, too. Finally in 1966, Edwin "Buzz" Aldrin Jr. walked in space for an incredible five hours!

That same year, NASA began **Lunar** Orbiter missions. The orbiters photographed safe moon-landing sites. From 1966 to 1968, NASA launched seven Surveyor missions. The Surveyors were the first U.S. spacecraft to land on the moon.

NASA knew its astronauts could survive in space long enough for a lunar mission. NASA also had pictures of good

During this moonwalk, Aldrin described his surroundings as a "magnificent desolation." Aldrin was the second man on the moon. When Armstrong took the first step on the moon, his famous words were, "That's one small step for man, one giant leap for mankind."

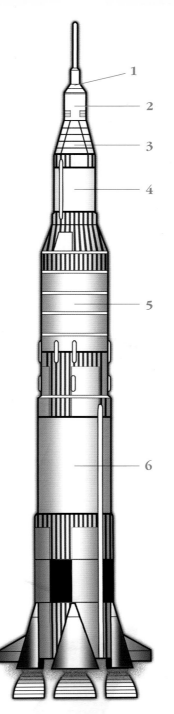

## SATURN V LAUNCH ROCKET AND APOLLO 11 SPACECRAFT

Wernher von Braun and his team developed the *Saturn V* launch rocket. The rocket was created to break through Earth's gravity. *Saturn V* had three parts called stages. The first two stages powered the craft into space. The third stage pushed the craft out of Earth's orbit.

The Apollo craft attached to the *Saturn V* had three parts, too. The service module provided the craft with electricity and oxygen. The astronauts lived in the command module, which later docked with the lunar module. And, the command module brought the astronauts home.

## THE *APOLLO 11* SPACECRAFT

### 1. Command Module (CM)
Contains crew's living area and all flight controls

### 2. Service Module (SM)
Contains *Apollo 11*'s electrical power supply and main rocket

### 3. Lunar Module (LM) *Eagle*
Flies lunar explorers to the moon. The ascent stage carries them back.

## THE *SATURN V* LAUNCH ROCKET

### 4. Third Stage
Places *Apollo 11* in orbit and sends it on its 3-day flight to the moon. Has 1 engine with 200,000 pounds (90,719 kg) of thrust and a life span of 8 minutes.

### 5. Second Stage
Contains 5 engines with a total thrust of 1 million pounds (453,592 kg). They can lift *Apollo 11* to 115 miles (185 km) above Earth at more than 15,000 miles per hour (24,140 km/h).

### 6. First Stage
Contains 5 engines with a combined thrust of 7.6 million pounds (3.4 million kg). This is the first stage to ignite. Its engines can reach a speed of 6,000 miles per hour (9,656 km/h), boosting *Apollo 11* to 40 miles (64 km) above Earth in 2.5 minutes.

moon-landing sites. And, it had actually landed craft on the moon. The United States was ready to meet President Kennedy's challenge and win the space race.

## Project Gemini

The Gemini program used the findings from the Mercury program to get one step closer to landing on the moon. Gemini took the Mercury craft and expanded on it. NASA also learned valuable skills that would be used to get to the moon.

On June 3, 1965, Edward White II was the first American to walk in space on *Gemini 4*. *Gemini 5* orbited Earth 120 times. Its astronauts stayed in space eight days. *Gemini 7* spent 14 days in space and made the first rendezvous. In all, the Gemini program had ten successful two-person missions.

# *Project Apollo*

An emblem honoring the Apollo 1
astronauts who lost their lives

NASA began the Apollo program to reach the goal of sending a man to the moon. First, NASA had to build a craft powerful enough to reach the moon and return to Earth.

On January 27, 1967, three astronauts prepared to test Apollo command and service **modules**. Suddenly, intense fire engulfed the craft. There was no way for the men to escape. All three died in the fire.

The accident delayed missions almost two years. The NASA review board determined the cause of the accident. Flammable parts and no emergency escape hatch on the craft caused the tragedy. NASA named the test *Apollo 1* in honor of the astronauts' sacrifice.

The Apollo program continued. Finally in October 1968, *Apollo* 7 orbited Earth. It was the first manned Apollo mission. Then on December 21, Apollo 8 became the first mission to orbit the moon.

NASA was closing in on the president's goal. The next step was landing a craft on the moon. Successful testing during Apollo 9 and 10 assured NASA that a moon landing was near.

On July 16, 1969, *Apollo 11* launched from Kennedy Space Center. On July 20, the **lunar module** *Eagle* landed on the moon. Astronaut Neil Armstrong made the first human footprint on the moon's surface. NASA had reached President Kennedy's goal. The United States had won the space race!

NASA continued with the Apollo program. *Apollo 13* was to be the third moon landing. The craft launched on April 11, 1970. However 55 hours into the flight, an oxygen tank in the service module exploded. The command module had no electricity or oxygen.

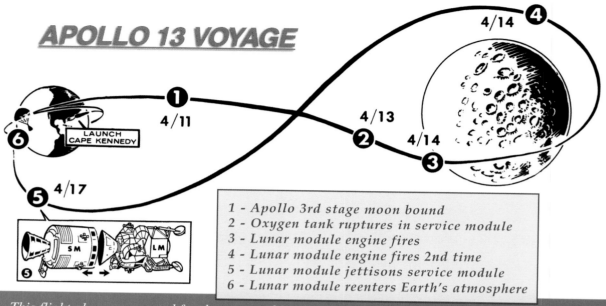

# APOLLO 13 VOYAGE

4/14

4/11

LAUNCH
CAPE KENNEDY

4/13

4/14

4/17

SM     LM

1 - Apollo 3rd stage moon bound
2 - Oxygen tank ruptures in service module
3 - Lunar module engine fires
4 - Lunar module engine fires 2nd time
5 - Lunar module jettisons service module
6 - Lunar module reenters Earth's atmosphere

*This flight plan was created for the return of Apollo 13 while the spacecraft was still moon bound.*

So, astronauts James Lovell, John Swigert Jr., and Fred Haise Jr. moved to the **lunar module**. They worked with Mission Control to return to Earth. The astronauts made it back to Earth on April 17. The world was relieved the astronauts were safe.

In January 1971, *Apollo 14* landed on the moon and completed *Apollo 13*'s mission. Astronauts brought more than 100 pounds (45 kg) of moon rock to Earth. They spent the longest time on the moon and took the longest moonwalk.

Also in 1971, *Apollo 15* astronauts were the first to ride across the moon in a **lunar rover**. On April 16, 1972, *Apollo 16* took off into space. Its astronauts were the first to take photos with an **ultraviolet** camera.

The Apollo program was doing well. The United States had put the first man on the moon. It had won the space race. And, scientists were studying the rocks, dust, and images the astronauts brought back to Earth.

The lunar rover allowed astronauts to explore more land than would have been possible on foot.

But times had changed. The United States was involved in the **Vietnam War**. And, the country's **economy** was weak. After the Apollo accidents, some thought the benefits of space travel were not worth the risks. So, Apollo 17 was the last manned mission to the moon.

# *Space Shuttles*

The Apollo program had ended. NASA's attention turned to facilities where people could live and work in space. But, NASA still needed a craft to carry people and equipment into space. The Apollo spacecraft had worked well. However, since only the command **module** returned to Earth, it was very expensive.

To save money, NASA worked to develop a reusable craft. It began a program called the Space Transportation System (STS). Craft created in this program became known as space shuttles.

On April 12, 1981, NASA launched space shuttle *Columbia* from the Kennedy Space Center. *Columbia* landed 54 hours later at California's Edwards Air Force Base. It had orbited Earth 36 times!

On January 28, 1986, space shuttle *Challenger* flew up into the clear blue sky. Seventy-three seconds later, the craft exploded.

*The 1986* Challenger *launch was delayed five times because of cold weather. This was to be the tenth flight of the* Challenger *orbiter.*

All seven crew members were killed, including S. Christa McAuliffe. McAuliffe had been the first teacher in space.

President Ronald Reagan formed the Rogers Commission to determine the cause of the accident. It found that a pressure seal had failed. This allowed hot gases to leak through a joint and ignite the craft's fuel. This failure was due to a faulty design.

*The* Challenger *crew*

Ellison Onizuka

S. Christa McAuliffe

Gregory Jarvis

Judith Resnik

Michael Smith

Francis "Dick" Scobee

Ronald McNair

NASA took almost three years to redesign the space shuttle. On September 29, 1988, the program resumed when *Discovery* was launched.

Next, NASA launched several **probes** to learn more about Venus, Jupiter, and the sun. In April 1990, *Discovery* launched the Hubble Space Telescope into orbit. Nine years later, the Chandra **X-ray** Observatory was launched. This telescope took X-rays of space!

Meanwhile, the shuttle program was running smoothly. On January 16, 2003, NASA launched space shuttle *Columbia*. The mission went as planned, and the crew completed 80 experiments.

On February 1, 2003, *Columbia* reentered Earth's atmosphere. Suddenly, it broke apart. All seven astronauts were killed. Again, NASA worked to determine the cause of a space shuttle accident.

The Columbia Accident Investigation Board determined what went wrong. During liftoff, a piece of insulation had broken off and hit the left wing. This increased the structural heat and destroyed the shuttle. After the accident, NASA suspended the space shuttle project.

## Space Shuttles

- **Atlantis**
- **Challenger**
- **Columbia**
- **Discovery**
- **Endeavour**
- **Enterprise**

The names of these space shuttle orbiters came from early sea vessels that reached new heights in research and exploration. *Endeavour* was actually chosen from a list of names submitted by schoolchildren from around the world.

The first shuttle, *Enterprise*, was originally going to be named Constitution. However, *Star Trek* viewers began a write-in campaign to name the craft *Enterprise*. The *Enterprise* was built as a test craft. The first orbiter to be used in space was *Columbia*.

# *Beyond the Moon*

NASA had worked hard to send astronauts into space. It had also been using unmanned craft to improve communication and explore the solar system.

In 1958, NASA launched Signal Communication by Orbiting Relay Experiment (SCORE). SCORE broadcast President Eisenhower's voice by **satellite**. It was the first communication of its kind. NASA later launched weather and television satellites.

NASA began exploring other planets in 1958 with the Pioneer program. Pioneer craft explored Jupiter, Saturn, and Venus. In the 1960s, the Mariner program sent unmanned craft to Venus and Mercury. *Mariner 4* took the first close-up pictures of Mars. And, *Mariner 9* mapped the planet's surface.

In 1975, NASA launched *Viking 1* and *Viking 2*. The two craft searched for life on Mars. In 1977, the *Voyager 1* and *Voyager 2* craft studied Jupiter and Saturn. They performed so well that NASA sent them to gather data from Uranus and Neptune, too.

**Each of these images was taken by different spacecraft.**

*From top to bottom is Mercury, Venus, Earth (and moon), Mars, Jupiter, Saturn, Uranus, and Neptune.*

*No spacecraft have visited Pluto yet. So, Pluto is not pictured.*

In 1992, the *Mars Observer* was launched to study Mars. It was supposed to be gone for an entire Martian year, or 687 Earth days. But in 1993, NASA lost the craft as it was about to go into orbit around Mars.

In 1997, the *Mars Pathfinder* landed on Mars. It took more than 16,000 pictures, analyzed rocks, and gathered weather information. That same year, the *Mars Global Surveyor* made a new map of the Martian surface.

NASA launched the *Mars Climate Orbiter* in 1998. Then in 1999, *Mars Polar Lander* was sent up. These two **probes** were intended to study Mars's weather and surface conditions. But NASA lost both craft.

On April 7, 2001, the *2001 Mars Odyssey* was launched. Its mission was to map the surface of the planet. It would also look for water and ice below the surface.

On January 3, 2004, the *Spirit* **rover** landed on Mars. It began sending information back immediately. Then on January 21, problems started. The rover stopped communicating with Mission Control. But, NASA soon fixed the craft. Today, *Spirit* continues to expand our knowledge of the Red Planet.

*This rover is similar to* Spirit, *which landed on Mars in 2004.*

# Today and Tomorrow

NASA continues its commitment to exploring space and expanding our knowledge of the solar system. The *Cassini* **probe** was launched in 1997. It began broadcasting images of Saturn in 2004. NASA is also working with other nations to build the International **Space Station**.

Americans understand the importance of space exploration. They appreciate the knowledge NASA has provided and wish to build on its success in the future. On January 14, 2004, President George W. Bush announced the Vision for Space Exploration.

In this program, a crew exploration vehicle will be developed by 2008. This craft will replace the space shuttle. The International Space Station will be complete by 2010. That same year, the space shuttle will be retired. And, NASA will develop outposts on the moon by 2020.

NASA's astronauts, scientists, and engineers have overcome problems with politics and finances. They have solved complex

*The International Space Station is also known as Alpha.*

problems and have suffered incredible loss. But, there is no doubt that NASA will again rise to meet a president's challenge.

# Glossary

**aeronautics** - a science dealing with the design, manufacture, and operation of aircraft.

**Cold War** - a period of tension and hostility between the United States and its allies and the Soviet Union and its allies after World War II.

**dock** - to join two spacecraft while in space.

**economy** - the way a nation uses its money, goods, and natural resources.

**lunar** - of or relating to the moon.

**module** - a self-contained unit or a part of a spacecraft that has a specific function.

**probe** - a device used to explore and send back information.

**rendezvous** - the process of bringing two spacecraft together.

**rover** - a vehicle used by astronauts to explore the surface of planets.

**satellite** - a manufactured object that orbits another object.

**space station** - a station in space that astronauts use for observation and as a launching pad.

**ultraviolet** - a type of light that cannot be seen with the human eye.

**Vietnam War** - from 1957 to 1975. A long, failed attempt by the United States to stop North Vietnam from taking over South Vietnam.

**X-ray** - a photograph taken by rays that can pass through substances that light cannot.

# *Web Sites*

To learn more about NASA, visit ABDO Publishing Company on the World Wide Web at **www.abdopub.com**. Web sites about NASA are featured on our Book Links page. These links are routinely monitored and updated to provide the most current information available.

# Index